100 QUESTIONS about OUTER SPACE

and all the answers too!

Written and Illustrated by
Simon Abbott

 PETER PAUPER PRESS, INC.
White Plains, New York

PETER PAUPER PRESS

In 1928, at the age of twenty-two, Peter Beilenson began printing books on a small press in the basement of his parents' home in Larchmont, New York. Peter—and later, his wife, Edna—sought to create fine books that sold at "prices even a pauper could afford."

Today, still family owned and operated, Peter Pauper Press continues to honor our founders' legacy of quality, value, and fun for big kids and small kids alike.

For Jack, Nathan, and Alfie,
who are out of this world.

Designed by Heather Zschock

Text and illustrations copyright © 2018 by Simon Abbott

Published by Peter Pauper Press, Inc.
202 Mamaroneck Avenue
White Plains, New York 10601 USA

Published in the United Kingdom and Europe by Peter Pauper Press, Inc.
c/o White Pebble International
Unit 2, Plot 11 Terminus Rd.
Chichester, West Sussex PO19 8TX, UK

Library of Congress Cataloging-in-Publication Data
Names: Abbott, Simon, 1967- author, illustrator.
Title: 100 questions about outer space : and all the answers, too! /
written and illustrated by Simon Abbott.
Other titles: One hundred questions about outer space
Description: White Plains, New York : Peter Pauper Press, Inc., [2018] |
Series: 100 questions | Audience: Ages 6-10. | Audience: K to grade 3.
Identifiers: LCCN 2017050149 | ISBN 9781441326171 (pbk. : alk. paper)
Subjects: LCSH: Astronomy--Miscellanea--Juvenile literature. | Children's
questions and answers. | Outer space--Miscellanea--Juvenile literature.
Classification: LCC QB46 .A23 2018 | DDC 520.2--dc23 LC record available at https://lccn.loc.
gov/2017050149
ISBN 978-1-4413-2617-1
Manufactured for Peter Pauper Press, Inc.
Printed in China

7 6

THIS IS EARTH CALLING!

Are you ready for a mind-boggling trip through the universe?

Discover the secrets of the solar system on a rocket-fueled adventure, speeding from planet to planet.

Which planet is the hottest? How big is the moon's largest crater? How long would it take you to fly to Pluto?

You'll check out space exploration and learn what's in store for the astronauts of the future!

Could one of those astronauts be you?

5...4...3...2...1...

BLAST OFF!

THE BIG BANG!

Have you ever looked up to the stars and wondered,
"How did the universe begin?"
Smart scientists have some ideas!

Can you tell me about the Big Bang?
Is it like when I get grumpy and slam the door?
Not really. It's when the universe first burst onto the scene! It suddenly got bigger and bigger very fast—and it's still getting bigger today. Before the Big Bang, scientists believe that the entire universe was a tiny point, thousands of times smaller than a pinhead.

When did this happen?
The Big Bang took place nearly 14 billion years ago. Once it started to grow, the universe doubled in size 90 times in a fraction of a second!

What's in the middle of the universe?

the letter V!

FACT or FICTION?
Were stars and planets formed right away?
No. At first, the universe was made up of just energy and matter.

What is energy?

Energy is what we need to get things done. It comes in many types, including heat, light, chemical, and nuclear energy. We use some form of energy in everything we do.

What is matter?

Matter is everything that takes up space. It can be our bodies, the air we breathe, or the food we eat. Matter is made of tiny particles called **atoms**. Matter takes different shapes, depending on how atoms are put together.

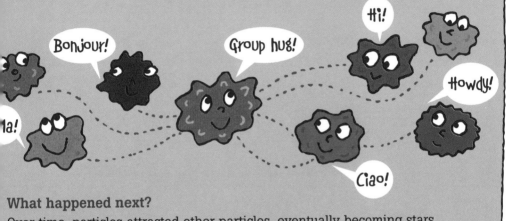

What happened next?

Over time, particles attracted other particles, eventually becoming stars, planets, and galaxies.

How much has the universe grown since the Big Bang?

Space today is billions of times bigger than it was when the universe was young, and is still expanding. Yowzah!

GLITTERING GALAXIES AND THE MAGICAL MILKY WAY!

What have we discovered about our own galaxy and the space beyond?

What are galaxies, anyway?
They're clusters of stars, gas, dust, and dark matter bound together by gravity.

I've heard of gravity. What does it do?
It's a force that pulls objects towards each other, a bit like a magnet. It's been around since the beginning of the universe. Earth's gravity keeps you on the ground, so you don't float away. Cool!

FACT OR FICTION?

Does the universe contain just one galaxy?
No—there are billions! Some are small, with only a few million stars. Our own galaxy has 200 billion stars, the oldest of which is about 13.4 billion years old. That's a lot of candles on its birthday cake!

Does our galaxy have a name?
Yes. It's called the Milky Way.

Why is it called that? Was there a stargazer addicted to chocolate?
No! It comes from the ancient Greeks, who called our galaxy "galaxias kyklos," which means "milky circle," because it looks like a milky white arc of light in the night sky.

How big is the Milky Way?
MASSIVE! NASA (the American government agency that explores space) estimates that the Milky Way is 100,000 light years across. That may sound huge, but it's a small-fry compared to the IC 1101 galaxy, which is 4 million light years wide!

What's a light year, anyway?
Scientists use the speed of light to measure HUGE distances in space. A light year is the distance light travels in one year, which is 5.88 TRILLION miles (9.5 trillion km).

What have we found out about other galaxies?
In the 1920s, the American astronomer Edwin Hubble proved that there were galaxies beyond our Milky Way. He found that the farther away a galaxy is, the faster it appears to move, because the universe is expanding. This is called Hubble's Law.

That's out of this world! What else can we thank Hubble for?
Hubble also identified the three main types of galaxies:

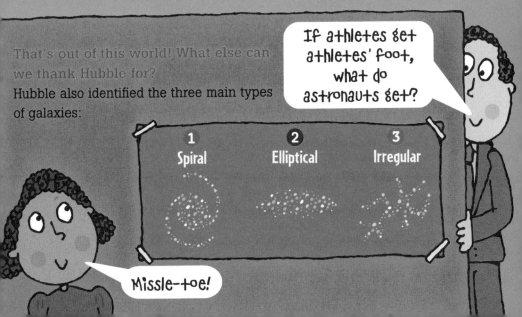

If athletes get athletes' foot, what do astronauts get?

Missle-toe!

1 Spiral
2 Elliptical
3 Irregular

STARGAZING AND SUN WORSHIPPING!

People have investigated the mysteries of the universe throughout history. Let's check out what our fellow earthlings discovered.

Does stargazing for science have a name?
Yes! The study of space is called **astronomy**. A scientist who does this is an **astronomer**.

How long have earth dwellers been doing this?
Astronomy is one of the world's oldest sciences. Humans have wanted to understand the moon, planets, and stars for thousands of years.

Who were some amazing early astronomers?
Records from ancient Chinese astronomy date back more than 4,000 years. They kept a record of every star they saw in the sky, and were the first civilization to describe Halley's Comet. Halley's Comet is an object made of ice and dust, with a tail of gas, that travels around the sun and is only visible from Earth every 75 years.

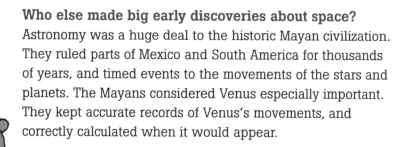

Who else made big early discoveries about space?
Astronomy was a huge deal to the historic Mayan civilization. They ruled parts of Mexico and South America for thousands of years, and timed events to the movements of the stars and planets. The Mayans considered Venus especially important. They kept accurate records of Venus's movements, and correctly calculated when it would appear.

Could ancient Egyptians predict events by studying the night sky?
Yes! When the brightest star in the sky, Sirius, rose before the sun, the Nile River would flood. This event marked the beginning of their calendar. (And would also mean they had soggy feet!)

What did the astronomers in ancient India discover?
A lot! They figured out that the sun is actually a star, and followed the movements of five planets. The astronomer Aryabhata was a genius! Born over 1,500 years ago, he calculated Earth's size almost perfectly.

How did old-time astronomers look at the stars?
The oldest stargazers looked up at the night sky with their naked eyes. A Dutch eyeglass maker, Hans Lippershey, probably invented the original telescope in 1608. However, the first astronomer to study the sky with a telescope was an Italian physicist named Galileo. In 1610, he discovered Jupiter's four biggest moons.

Last night in bed I was gazing at the stars and thinking to myself . . .
. . . where the heck is my roof?!

MIND-BLOWING MODERN MISSIONS

We've sent unmanned spacecraft to explore the solar system and beyond!

MISSION 1 *LAUNCHED 1977*

SPACECRAFT NAME?
Voyager 1 and *Voyager 2*
(They are twin robotic spacecraft.)

GOING TO?
Both Voyagers flew by and photographed Jupiter and Saturn.
Voyager 2 then investigated Uranus and Neptune. In 2012,
Voyager 1 became the first spacecraft to leave the solar system!

ANY COOL FACTS?
Both craft carry gold-plated disks with greetings from Earth.
The disks include images, music, and messages in 55 languages.

ANY DISCOVERIES?
Voyager 2 discovered rings around Uranus and 10 new moons.
It also sighted a stormy "Great Dark Spot" on Neptune!

MISSION 2 *LAUNCHED 1997*

SPACECRAFT NAME?
Cassini-Huygens

GOING TO?
Saturn. It took 7 years to get there, traveling
2.2 billion miles (3.5 billion km).

WHEN DID THE MISSION END?
In September 2017, *Cassini* went out with a bang. It flew past Saturn's biggest
moon, Titan, then dove between Saturn and its icy rings. At last, *Cassini*
dropped into Saturn's atmosphere and burned up, sending information back
to Earth until it was destroyed.

ANY DISCOVERIES?
Cassini-Huygens found evidence of a giant ocean on a frozen moon called
Enceladus. It also got the low-down on methane lakes on Saturn's biggest
moon, Titan.

MISSION 3 *LAUNCHED 2009*

SPACECRAFT NAME?
Kepler

GOING TO?
The universe!

WHAT WAS THE COST?
$600 million

HOW BIG IS THE SPACECRAFT?
It's 9 feet wide and 15.3 feet high (2.7 m wide and 4.7 m high). That's as tall as a giraffe!

AIM OF THE MISSION?
To survey the galaxy and look for Earth-sized planets that people might be able to live on.

ANY DISCOVERIES?
Kepler has spotted over 2,300 new planets in other galaxies, more than 20 of which might have basic similarities to Earth!

MISSION 4 *LAUNCHED 2011*

SPACECRAFT NAME?
Juno (named after the wife of the Roman god Jupiter)

GOING TO?
Jupiter. It took five years to get there!

HOW BIG IS THE SPACECRAFT?
It measures 66 feet (20 m) across—the height of a six-story building.

ANY AMAZING FACTS?
Juno will orbit Jupiter 37 times to learn about how the planet was formed and what it's like on the gas giant today. It will collect information using everything from a color camera to magnetometers.

What is the International Space Station?

It's a flying space laboratory, launched in 1998. 16 countries have worked together to build it, including the USA, Russia, Japan, Canada, and 11 members of the European Space Agency.

How big is the International Space Station?

It's the biggest human-made object in space! It's larger than a six-bedroom house.

How many astronauts can live there?

Six people can check in! It has a gym and two bathrooms, and they can keep an eye on Earth through a big bay window.

> What happened to the astronaut who stepped on chewing gum?

How long do astronauts stay there?

Missions usually last about six months. Scott Kelly (U.S.) and Mikhail Kornienko (Russia) hold the record for the longest stay. They lived on board for 340 days!

How fast does the International Space Station circle Earth?

Approximately 16 times a day. That means record holders Kelly and Kornienko whirled around Earth a mind-blowing 5,440 times. Bet they were dizzy!

VIQ (Very Important Question)! What happens when the Space Station crew visit the bathroom?

To keep from floating away, the crew fix themselves to the toilet using leg restraints. Astronauts save water by purifying and recycling pee into drinking water. Poop gets ejected and burns up in the atmosphere like shooting stars.

Where do they sleep?

Each astronaut has a sleeping bag attached to a wall or ceiling. Lack of gravity means they snore less, too! Peace at last!

What do the crew eat?

Astronauts choose their meals before they blast off on a mission. They note what they eat on one of the station's 52 computers to make sure they get a balanced diet. Food is delivered by the *ATV* (Automatic Transfer Vehicle), an unmanned cargo spacecraft. Wonder if it delivers pizza?

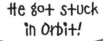

He got stuck in Orbit!

What do the astronauts work on in space?

Among other things, science experiments! Some crews study the effects of space on animals, including ants, squid, mice, and flatworms. They also work on projects like 3D printing, robotics, and how fire burns in zero gravity.

Do the astronauts go on spacewalks?

Yes! The crew put on their spacesuits, which provide oxygen and water, and head outside. They can attach to the Space Station with tethers, and can balance on the robotic arm to do experiments and repairs. Amazing!

COOL CONSTELLATIONS!

What is a star?
It's a huge, burning ball of gas.

How do stars shine?
At the center of the star, hydrogen atoms smash together, creating helium. This gives off energy, making the star shine. A star dies when the hydrogen runs out.

What is the brightest star in Earth's sky?
The winner is **Sirius**, which means "glowing" in Greek, and it's actually two stars that look like one from far away. The largest known star is **UY Scuti**. It's about five billion times bigger than the sun!

What's a constellation?
It's a group of stars that, when viewed from Earth, form a pattern. Constellations can look like animals, objects, and even legendary characters!

How many constellations are there?
Modern astronomers have split up the sky into 88 official constellations. There are more star patterns, though, seen and named by different cultures.

Are constellations useful?
Yes! They let people recognize stars in the sky. Throughout history, star patterns have helped people keep track of the calendar, letting them know when to plant and harvest crops. Sailors used constellations for navigation. Ship ahoy!

What are some famous constellations?

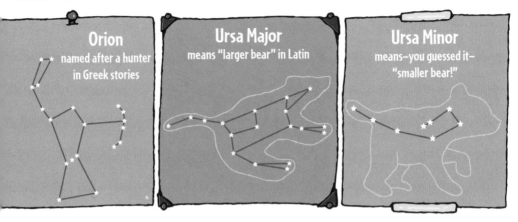

Orion
named after a hunter
in Greek stories

Ursa Major
means "larger bear" in Latin

Ursa Minor
means—you guessed it—
"smaller bear!"

Would I see the same constellations everywhere in the world?

No. You see different parts of the sky from different places on the globe.
Your view also changes with the seasons. If you're south of the equator, you
may spot the **Emu** pattern of stars and nebulae (space clouds) or the **Crux**.
The Crux is the smallest official constellation, but also one of the brightest!

Crux

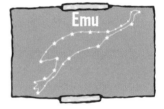

Emu

How can I spot a constellation?

If you can, grab a telescope or binoculars. A red flashlight would be useful,
because bright white light affects your night vision. A compass will tell you
which direction you're facing. Finally, get a star chart or star-finding app.

Where should I go?

Pick a clear night, away from tall buildings and bright lights. (The middle of a
park might be good.) Let your eyes adjust to the darkness. Locate north with
your compass and compare what you see to your star chart. Always have an
adult with you when you go stargazing!

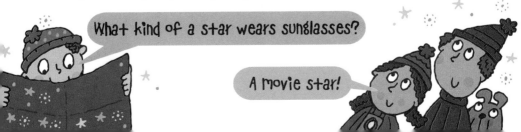

What kind of a star wears sunglasses?

A movie star!

SENSATIONAL SOLAR SYSTEM!

Can you name the eight planets (and a famous dwarf planet) in our solar system? Here are the worlds that share our sun!

What is the solar system?

It's the collection of planets, moons, comets, asteroids, dust, and gas that travel around (orbit) the sun. Planets are the eight largest objects orbiting the sun.

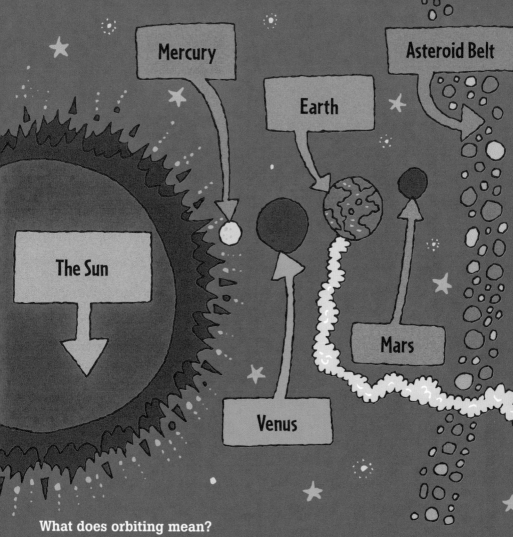

Mercury

Earth

Asteroid Belt

The Sun

Mars

Venus

What does orbiting mean?

It's basically an object circling round another object. Johannes Kepler, a 17th century German astronomer, figured out how planets orbit the Sun in an oval (or elliptical) shape.

Are these orbiting objects like pebbles on a beach?
Think bigger! They can range from a few feet to hundreds
of miles across. (Smaller space rocks are meteoroids, and any
space rocks that fall to Earth are meteorites.) Vesta is one of the largest
asteroids. It is 326 miles wide (524 km) and features a mountain twice the
size of Mount Everest. Wow!

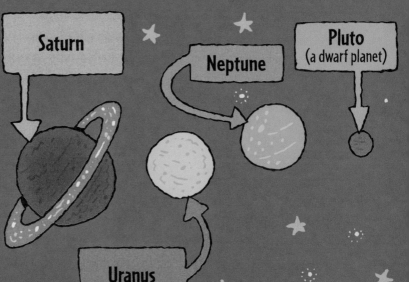

Saturn

Neptune

Pluto
(a dwarf planet)

Uranus

Jupiter

**Why does everything in the solar system rotate
around the sun?**
The sun is SO huge and heavy that its gravity pulls all
the other objects into orbit around it. This gigantic gas
ball is 300,000 times heavier than Earth!

What kind of dishes
do they use in space?

Back up a little! What are comets and asteroids?
A comet is a large ball of rock and ice. As it flies close to
the sun, it gives off a "tail" of dust and gas. An asteroid is
an orbiting chunk of rock and metal.

Flying saucers!

What are the planets in our solar system?

Let's start with the different types of planets. The first set have hard rocky surfaces, and are called **terrestrial planets**. This group is known as the **inner solar system**, and includes **Mercury**, **Venus**, **Earth**, and **Mars**.

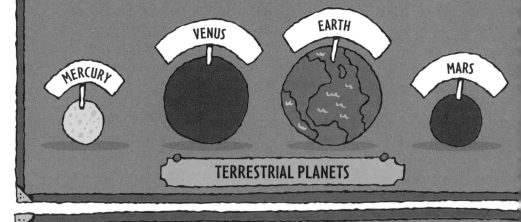

TERRESTRIAL PLANETS

What types of planets are in the outer solar system?

They're made of layers of gas and liquid, around a hot core.

What are these big gassy planets called?

Because of their enormous size, **Jupiter**, **Saturn**, **Uranus**, and **Neptune** are **gas giants**. The inner and outer solar systems are separated by the **asteroid belt** (which is what it sounds like: a big hoop of asteroids and other stuff).

What about Pluto?

Pluto is a dwarf planet, mostly made of rock and ice.

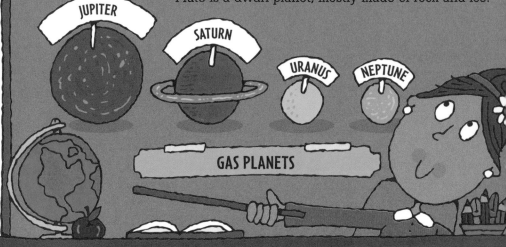

GAS PLANETS

How big is the solar system?

H-U-G-E! The end of the system is about 122 astronomical units (AU) from the Sun. One AU is 93 million miles (150 million km). If you could hop on a plane and head for Pluto, it would take you 700 years to get there. Go grab your passport!

Is there a simple way to remember the order of the planets?

Sure! Check this out.

My	Very	Enormous	Machine
Mercury	**Venus**	**Earth**	**Mars**

Just	Scooped	Up	Noodles
Jupiter	**Saturn**	**Uranus**	**Neptune**

HERE COMES THE SUN!

Without this scorching ball of gas, life on Earth would be toast.

Aside from "big and bright," what is the sun?

The sun is the star at the center of our solar system. It feels much brighter and hotter than other stars because it is closer to us.

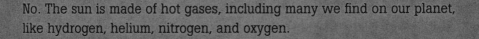

Does the sun have a rocky surface like Earth?

No. The sun is made of hot gases, including many we find on our planet, like hydrogen, helium, nitrogen, and oxygen.

SUPER SUN!

How big is the sun?
The sun is ENORMOUS! You might think it looks tiny, but that's because it's 93 million miles (150 million km) away!

Could you just answer the question?
Yes, of course! The sun is 865,000 miles (1,400,000 km) wide. For comparison, Earth is 7,900 miles (12,725 km) across.

Why didn't the sun go to the university?

Because she already had a million degrees!

YOU ARE HERE!

Sometimes the sun feels scorching here on Earth. Just how warm does it get?

The sun gets VERY hot! The temperature inside the sun can hit a mind-boggling 27 million°F (15 million °C). The "surface" of the sun is the part we see, and reaches a cool 10,000°F (5,538°C). Toasty!

Has the sun been around for a while?
How old is this gas ball?

The sun is over 4.6 billion years old. That's a lot of birthdays!

FACT
FICTION

Would we still be able to live on Earth without the sun?

No. We need the sun to survive. If it vanished, within a week, Earth's temperature would drop below zero °F (-18°C), and plummet to -100°F (-73°C) after a year. The top layer of the oceans would freeze, trees would die, and animals that rely on plants for food would become extinct. Eventually, life on Earth would be impossible. Let's hear it for the sun!

What about solar eclipses?

The moon travels around Earth once a month. An eclipse happens if the moon lines up exactly between Earth and the sun, blocking the sunlight for a few minutes.

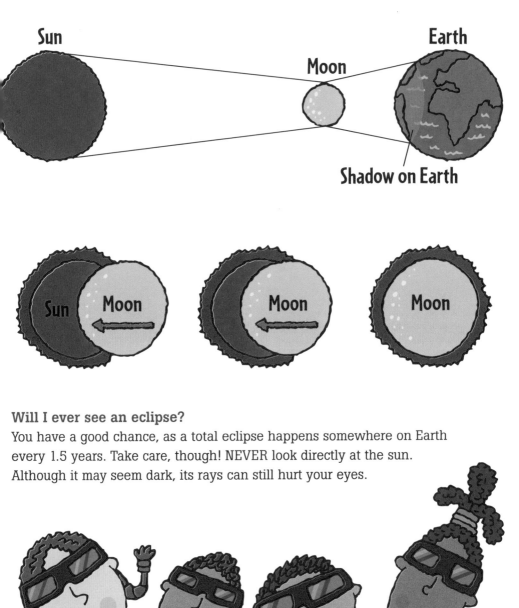

Will I ever see an eclipse?

You have a good chance, as a total eclipse happens somewhere on Earth every 1.5 years. Take care, though! NEVER look directly at the sun. Although it may seem dark, its rays can still hurt your eyes.

23

THE POCKET-SIZED PLANET!

Mini Mercury may be small, but it's speedy!

Mercury is the closest planet to the Sun. Does this mean that it's scorching hot?
Yes! You'd need sunscreen with a daily high of 800°F (427°C)! At night the temperatures dip down to a freezing -290°F (-179°C). Brrrr!

Why are Mercury's nights so cold?
It doesn't have much atmosphere to keep the heat in. The planet is small, so its gravity is weak, and gases around it disappear into space.

Why is Mercury covered with craters?
It's the lack of atmosphere again! There isn't enough gas around the planet to give it much protection from falling space rocks.

How long is a year on Mercury?
It's your birthday before you know it on the solar system's speediest planet! A year is just 88 days long!

Do you like the new restaurant on Mercury?

the food is tasty, but there's not much atmosphere!

IT'S ALL RELATIVE!

Venus is often called Earth's sister planet!

What is Venus like? Can we see the planet's surface from Earth?

Venus is covered with clouds of sulfuric acid, so we can't sneak a peek. But space missions found that our sister planet is home to thousands and thousands of volcanos.

Is Venus the closest planet to Earth?

Yes! At an average distance of 25,476,219 miles (41 million km), Venus is our closest planetary neighbor!

Could we visit Venus?

It would be a tough trip! Temperatures are hot enough to melt lead, with a sizzling high of 864°F (462°C), and the air is unbreathable too!

Is Venus covered with craters like Mercury?

It has fewer craters than Mercury, because its thick atmosphere fries falling space rocks unless they're huge.

THERE'S NO PLACE LIKE HOME!

What makes our planet so unique? Earth's got a lot to offer!

What's Earth made of, anyway?
Earth is layered like an onion. We live on the surface layer, 71% of which is covered in water, mostly ocean. The land and bottom of the oceans form a rocky top layer called the crust, which is 3 to 44 miles (5 to 71 km) deep. The crust is split into huge rocky plates that float on the layer below: the **mantle**.

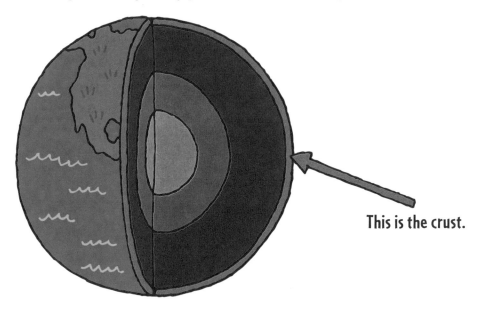

This is the crust.

The plates are floating! Does this mean they move around?
Yes! They constantly shift, moving anywhere from one to four inches (2.5 to 10 cm) a year.

What happens if they bump into each other?

When these floating plates push together, they can form mountains or volcanoes.

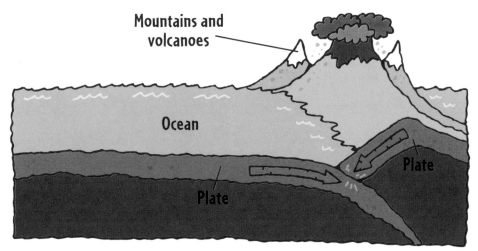

Earthquakes can happen when plates slide past each other.

If they are pulled apart, the separating plates can create valleys or lakes.

Let's go down a layer. Can you tell me about the mantle?
Sure! It's Earth's widest section and contains both solid rock and molten (or melted) rock called **magma**.

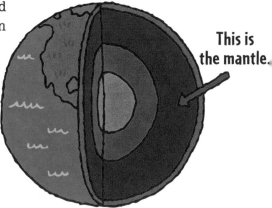

This is the mantle.

Here is the outer core.

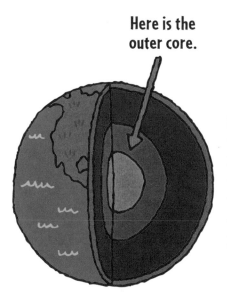

Next layer please! Have we reached the middle yet?
Not quite! Now we're at Earth's outer core. Geologists (scientists who study rocks) think this is a layer of liquid metal that constantly churns, creating the magnetic field that protects Earth.

Earth's center is called the inner core.

Are we there yet? What is the final layer called?
Welcome to Earth's inner core! Metals found here include gold, silver, and platinum, plus lots of iron and nickel. It can get as hot as the surface of the sun here. All that heat would normally melt the metals into liquid, but the inner core is pretty solid because the pressure at the planet's center is so intense.

Is Earth the only planet in our solar system with life?

It's true! Earth is just the right distance from the Sun, so temperatures are not too hot or cold. Most creatures need oxygen, and they get it from Earth's air and water. Our plants receive light from the sun, but Earth is protected from some of the sun's more dangerous rays by a part of our atmosphere called the ozone layer. Lucky us!

What did the crust say to the earthquake?

Does Earth REALLY spin?

It does! Earth rotates around an imaginary line, or axis, that passes through the North and South poles. The planet spins once every day, and reaches a speed of about 1,000 miles per hour (1,609 kph).

You crack me up!

That's super fast! Why don't we get dizzy or fall off?

You don't feel the world spinning because you and everything else on the planet are moving along with Earth. It's only if the planet suddenly stopped spinning that you'd know about it!

THE MAGNIFICENT MOON!

Take a small step and a giant leap to discover the mysteries of the moon, Earth's **satellite**!

The moon is our satellite? What's a satellite?

It's something that orbits a star or a planet. Earth orbits the sun, so it is a satellite. The moon is a satellite because it orbits Earth.

How does the man in the moon cut his hair?

Eclipse it!

How big is the moon?

The moon is about a quarter as big as Earth, and measures 6,783.5 miles (10,917 km) around!

Does the moon have seas?
Not true! Early scientists thought that the dark patches they could see from Earth were oceans. But actually, they are pools of hardened lava. Easy mistake to make!

Are there a lot of craters on the moon?
With almost no atmosphere to protect it, the moon has taken a battering. Meteors have created some impressive impacts, the South Pole–Aitken Basin being the largest. This dynamic dent measures 1,600 miles (2,575 km) across, and 5 miles (8 km) down. That's over 5 times deeper than the Grand Canyon!

Is the moon the only place humans have visited outside of Earth?
It's true! We first traveled there via Apollo 11, a mission that launched on July 16th, 1969, and reached the moon four days later.

Did everything go according to plan?
Not quite. Once in the moon's orbit, astronaut Michael Collins stayed in the main spacecraft, *Columbia*. The lunar lander, *Eagle*, was piloted by Neil Armstrong and Buzz Aldrin. On the way down to the moon's surface, *Eagle's* automatic landing system took them way off course, heading towards a rock-filled crater. With only 30 seconds of fuel left, Armstrong grabbed the controls, and managed to land on a flat plain. What a white-knuckle ride!

Who was the first person on the moon?
Neil Armstrong! His first words from the moon were, "That's one small step for Man, one giant leap for mankind." About 600 million people watched the landing on TV. Armstrong was soon joined by astronaut Buzz Aldrin.

What was one of their toughest tasks?
Planting the American flag! Studies suggested that the moon's surface was soft. In fact, it was hard rock covered with dust. They knocked the pole in, and filmed it quickly in case it fell over!

Besides the flag, did the crew from Apollo 11 leave anything behind?
The astronauts placed a sign on the moon with a message ending, "We come in peace for all mankind." They set up the Lunar Laser Ranging Experiment, which is still running today! It discovered that the moon has a fluid core, and is gradually moving away from Earth.

Can you still see the astronauts' footprints on the moon?
Yes! Next to no atmosphere means no wind, no rain, and nothing to wear them away. The famous prints are there to this day!

LIFE ON MARS?

This so-called Red Planet is our cool cosmic neighbor.

Why is Mars known as the Red Planet?
The iron minerals in its soil rust, causing the dusty surface to appear red.

FACT OR FICTION?

Is Mars named after a chocolate bar?
Nope! The ancient Romans named the fiery-colored planet after their god of war.

How is Mars like Earth?
Mars has polar ice caps, and water has been discovered in the form of ice, brine, and vapor. It has seasons, like Earth, and features such as canyons, volcanoes, and mountains.

**Sounds like a great place to visit!
Should I plan a vacation?**
Don't plan a trip yet! You would suffer from lack of oxygen
and freezing temperatures. Radiation and toxic soil are
also dangers.

What does Mars hold
up its pants with?

An asteroid belt!

**Ignoring those hazards, how long
would it take to get there?**
Probably about 160 days—pretty quick,
considering the trip would be roughly 140
million miles (225.3 million km). That's a long
way to pop back if you forget your toothbrush!

Have there been any missions to Mars?

Yes! Scientists have been sending unmanned spacecraft to Mars for over 50 years. Some flew by, taking photographs. Others orbited the planet, and some managed to land and explore. (Others crash-landed! Whoops!)

NASA launched the Viking project in 1975. It was the first U.S. mission to land on Mars and send back color photographs. It explored Mars for over six years and collected the first-ever sample of Martian dirt.

Briny flowing water might be found here!

Look! Iron-rich clay minerals!

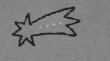

Are we still exploring and experimenting today?

We discover new stuff about the Red Planet all the time. The Mars Exploration Rovers were launched by NASA in 2003 to search for answers about water on Mars. They can travel up to 144 feet (44 meters) per day, and have robotic arms, cameras, X-rays, magnets, microscopes, and tools to break down rock.

Meteorites here!

What did we find out about Mars from the Rovers?

The Rovers have revealed large meteorites, iron-rich clay minerals, and signs that there might once have been liquid water on Mars. New discoveries are still being made!

Let's peek at Jupiter's impressive stats.

Is Jupiter the solar system's biggest planet?

It's true! Jupiter is as wide as 11.2 Earths side by side. You could fit 1,300 Earths inside it.

Is it heavy too?

Jupiter weighs twice as much as all the other planets in the solar system combined.

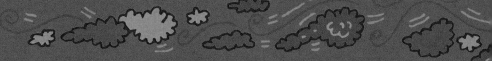

So Jupiter is a gas giant. What's it made of, and how do the gases stay together?

Jupiter is mostly hydrogen and helium. Ammonia clouds move across the surface, above colorful gases below. Pressure squashes the gases into liquids farther inside the planet.

What's at the planet's core?

No one is sure what Jupiter's core looks like, but the *Juno* spacecraft is helping us figure it out. The core's temperature could be seven times hotter than the surface of the sun. Yowzah!

What is Jupiter's Great Red Spot? Is treasure buried there?
Good guess, but no! It's a giant spinning hurricane. The storm is the size of Earth, and takes six Earth days just to rotate once!

Sounds ferocious. How does it compare with storms on Earth?
The strongest hurricanes on Earth are called Category 5, and the winds rage at up to 200 mph (321 kph). The Great Red Spot blows that speed away with jaw-dropping winds of 384 mph (618 kph).

Does Jupiter have a moon like Earth?
Yes! It's got more than 50! The four largest are called Europa, Callisto, Ganymede, and Io.

Because jupiter is so gassy!

Why is Earth glad to be so far away from jupiter?

Didn't that Galileo guy spot those moons with one of the first telescopes?
Yup!

LOOPS AND HOOPS!

Saturn's famous rings around the planet are made of ice and dust!

Is Saturn the only planet with rings?
No, although they are the most impressive! Jupiter, Uranus, and Neptune have rings too, but they're less showy.

How big are Saturn's rings?
The bands are incredibly thin—just 30 feet (9 meters) thick for the most part. However, they measure 175,000 miles (281,635 km) wide in places.

Who discovered the rings?
It's our old friend Galileo again! He saw them through his trusty telescope in 1610, but it took until 1655 for astronomer Christiaan Huygens to realize they were a disk. However, the native Maori people of New Zealand might have beaten them to it. They historically called Saturn "Parearau," an ancient word meaning "surrounded by a band."

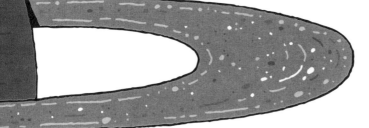

What did Mars say to Saturn?

Give me a ring sometime!

Could Saturn float in water?
It depends how big your bathtub is! Saturn is mainly made from the gases hydrogen and helium. It's light and less dense than water . . . so it would float!

FACT OR FICTION?

JUST CHILLING OUT!

Uranus is the coldest planet in the solar system. Bundle up!

Neptune is farthest away from the Sun, so how is "ice giant" Uranus the coldest planet?
It's a bitter battle! Neptune's average temperature falls to a frosty -350°F (-212°C), and Uranus records an average -315°F (-193°C). However, temperatures on Uranus have dropped to a finger-numbing -371°F (-224°C), the coldest of any planet. Take that, neighbor!

Is that why Uranus looks a little blue?
Nope! That's a trick of the light. Uranus's atmosphere contains methane, which reflects blue light back into space. That's why Uranus appears blue!

Does Uranus really rotate on its side?
More or less! It's the only sideways planet. This might be because a planet-sized object crashed into Uranus billions of years ago. Watch where you're going!

Why does Uranus have lots of friends?

Because it's so cool!

WILD AND WINDY!

Hold on to your hat! Stormy Neptune has the strongest winds in the solar system.

You said that storm speeds on Jupiter reach 384 mph (618 kph). How do Neptune's gales compare?
Winds roar across Neptune's skies at a supersonic 1,500 mph (2,414 kph). That's nearly eight times faster than the strongest hurricane on Earth!

Can you see Neptune without a telescope?
Nope! It's too far away.

How did scientists first find it, then?
When Neptune was finally spotted in 1846, it became the first planet ever discovered using math!

What? How can math find a planet?
Astronomers saw changes in Uranus's orbit. Mathematician Urbain le Verrier thought that these changes might be caused by an unknown planet nearby. He asked German astronomer Johann Gottfried Galle to search the sky for the planet. With help from his student, Johann spotted Neptune right where le Verrier's calculations said it would be!

What kind of songs do planets sing?

Nep-tunes!

DISMISSED AND DEMOTED!

Poor Pluto is a planet no more!
Let's find out about its fall from grace.

Why is Pluto not a planet any more?
Since its discovery in 1930, Pluto took its place as
the "last planet of the solar system." However, the
International Astronomical Union set new rules in
2006, which redefined Pluto as a dwarf planet.
Sounds like bad news!

Which planetary rule does Pluto break?
Yes … it's round! Yes … it orbits the sun! However, a planet must
"clear the neighborhood of its orbit." This means that as it travels,
its gravity must sweep away objects from the space around it.
Pluto does not do this, so it had to leave the planet club!

Mercury ✓   Venus ✓   Earth ✓   Mars ✓

Jupiter ✓   Saturn ✓   Uranus ✓   Neptune ✓   Pluto ✗

So, is Pluto surrounded by lots of space clutter?
Yes! Pluto is part of the Kuiper Belt beyond Neptune's orbit. This belt contains
tons of rock and ice. It's 3.67 billion miles (5.9 billion km) from the Sun, so
there isn't a lot of light, and it's hard to see even with the most powerful
telescopes.

43

BLAST OFF!

Strap yourself in for a journey through the history of space exploration!

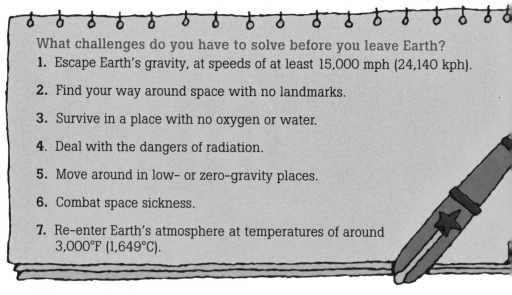

What challenges do you have to solve before you leave Earth?

1. Escape Earth's gravity, at speeds of at least 15,000 mph (24,140 kph).

2. Find your way around space with no landmarks.

3. Survive in a place with no oxygen or water.

4. Deal with the dangers of radiation.

5. Move around in low- or zero-gravity places.

6. Combat space sickness.

7. Re-enter Earth's atmosphere at temperatures of around 3,000°F (1,649°C).

What was the first rocket sent into space?
During World War II, the German V-2 A4 Rocket became the first to reach space.

Who was the first astronaut to blast off?
Hang on! First, scientists needed to see if space travel was safe for humans. Fruit flies were launched in 1947, and a monkey in 1949. The Russian dog Laika became the first animal to orbit Earth in 1957.

Okay, so now we've made spaceflight safe. Who was the first human in space?
Russian cosmonaut Yuri Gagarin spent 108 minutes orbiting Earth in April 1961, and became a world-wide star!

When did the first woman fly to space?
Just two years later, in 1963, skydiver and Russian cosmonaut Valentina Tereshkova blasted off. She was part of a 70-hour spaceflight that made a dazzling 48 orbits of Earth.

Did people start traveling to space more after that?
Yes, but it was really expensive, because early spacecraft could only be used once.

Yikes! Did they solve that problem?
In 1981, NASA launched its first reusable spacecraft, the space shuttle. It took off like a rocket, and returned to Earth like a glider. By its final flight in 2011, the Space Shuttle Program's five craft had flown 135 missions.

Did a space shuttle carry anything HUGE into space?
In 1990, the Space Shuttle *Discovery* launched the Hubble Space Telescope into orbit! The Hubble telescope has helped us understand how old the universe is and how planets are born.

Were Space Shuttle crews allowed to bring their pets?
No, but they did measure the effects of gravity (and the lack of gravity) on plants and animals. Ants, shrimp, bees, frogs, spiders, mice, snails, and fish are just a few of the creatures that hitched a ride in the Space Shuttle's laboratories!

What is an astronaut's favorite social network?

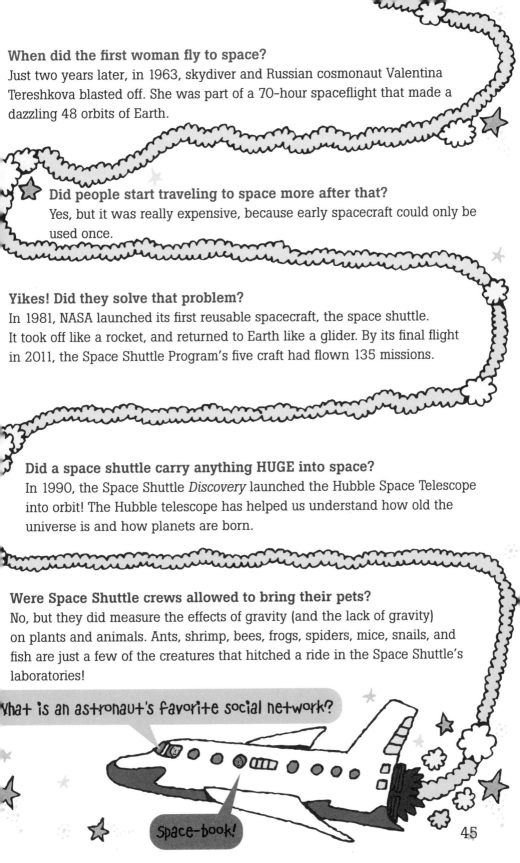

Space-book!

BLUE SKIES AHEAD!

What exciting plans do space experts have for the future? Could we all be checking in to the Mars Motel for our vacation?

I want to visit space! Can I? If so, when?
Probably, in a few years! A bunch of private companies are working on vehicles to send regular people into space. Seven space tourists have already hitched a ride on Russian flights to the International Space Station, and it's only a matter of time before the first paying passengers blast off.

| FLIGHT TIME | DESTINATION | GATE NUMBER |
| 17:45 | MOON | SPX7 |

I'm saving up my money for a ticket to space! How much will I need?
A lot! A tourist trip around the moon in the future will probably set you back millions of dollars.

What if I become an astronaut when I grow up? Where in space could I go?
Mars is the ultimate goal, and the European Space Agency is working on a manned mission to the Red Planet. Their target is a touchdown date in 2035, which gives you plenty of time!

Does NASA have anything planned?

Of course! The new *Orion* spacecraft will carry astronauts farther than ever before. It could travel to an asteroid in deep space, or even to Mars. *Orion* had an unmanned test flight in 2014, reaching 3,600 miles (5,794 km) above Earth. That's 14 times higher than the International Space Station!

Was the test a triumph?

Yes! The spacecraft survived high levels of radiation, speeds of 20,000 mph (32,187 kph) when re-entering Earth's atmosphere, and temperatures of 4,000°F (2,204°C). Its enormous parachutes slowed *Orion's* fall before "splashdown" in the Pacific Ocean. The first flight with a crew is pencilled in for 2021.

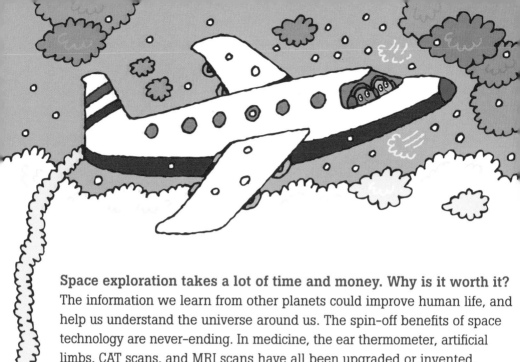

Space exploration takes a lot of time and money. Why is it worth it?
The information we learn from other planets could improve human life, and help us understand the universe around us. The spin-off benefits of space technology are never-ending. In medicine, the ear thermometer, artificial limbs, CAT scans, and MRI scans have all been upgraded or invented, thanks to space research. Other discoveries include anti-icing on airplanes, safer car tires, more protective firefighter uniforms, weather forecasting, and computer technology. Thanks, outer space!